P9-DBI-099

DANCE ★ CRAZY

Waltz

DANCE ★ CRAZY

Waltz

Paul Bottomer

LORENZ BOOKS

NEW YORK · LONDON · SYDNEY · BATH

793.33
607

This edition published in 1997 by Lorenz Books
27 West 20th Street, New York NY 10011

LORENZ BOOKS are available for bulk purchase
for sales promotion and for premium use.
For details, write or call the manager of special sales:
Lorenz Books, 27 West 20th Street,
New York NY 10011; (800) 354-9657

© 1997 Anness Publishing Limited

Lorenz Books is an imprint of
Anness Publishing Limited

All rights reserved. No part of this publication may be
reproduced, stored in a retrieval system, or transmitted in
any way or by any means, electronic, mechanical,
photocopying, recording or otherwise, without the
prior written permission of the copyright holder.

ISBN 1 85967 396 1

Publisher: Joanna Lorenz
Senior Editor: Lindsay Porter
Photographer: John Freeman
Clothes Stylist: Jackie Holland
Hair and Make-up: Karen Kennedy
Designer: Siân Keogh

Printed in China

1 3 5 7 9 10 8 6 4 2

12⁹⁵

Contents

Introduction

The Waltz has endured to this day as one of the favorite standard dances of all time. Whether it helps to start a new relationship with the evening's last dance or to celebrate a wedding or anniversary, the Waltz remains the only dance whose innate romance links it inextricably with life's happier moments. It is not surprising, then, that the Waltz is often the first standard dance encountered by newcomers to the exciting adventure of learning to dance.

When we look back at the origins of the Waltz, we discover a dance that has adapted in a remarkable way to changing fashions over the many decades of its two-century history. The dance destined to symbolize romance was born toward the end of the 18th century as nothing more sophisticated than an Austro-German folk dance called the Ländler. It was characterized by the rotary gyrations of men and women dancing together as partners. In the early years of the 19th century, the Waltz took the controversial step of adopting a hold in which the man's right hand was placed around the lady's waist. The great debate concerning the dubious morality of the Waltz continued for years. Then, the Russian czar Alexander gave the dance the royal seal of approval, when he was observed openly dancing and enjoying the Waltz in public. The enormous popularity of the Viennese Waltzes composed and played by the Strauss family throughout the latter half of the 19th century ensured that, by the century's end, the Waltz had reached its pinnacle of popularity.

By the time of World War I, a new generation of dancers was rebelling against the "old-time" feel of the Viennese Waltzes with their fast tempos and structured positions and looking for a more natural, less stylized way of dancing the Waltz. A revolution in the Waltz style had started to take place with the advent of another dance called the Boston, in which the dancers employed a "modern," closer hold, dancing hip-to-hip and at a more leisurely pace. Although the Boston itself had virtually disappeared by the outbreak of the war, it was to become one of the influences on the new-style Waltz.

Left: The Waltz has adapted to suit changing fashions over two centuries.

In 1914 the craze for the Foxtrot spread from America to Europe, overshadowing the Waltz, which was still perceived to have Germanic associations. In 1921, with the Waltz all but extinct, *The Dancing Times* called a conference of dance teachers in London to discuss many of the pressing issues of the day. One was the decline in popularity of the Waltz during the war and the confusion arising out of its lack of standard technique. From this conference came today's standard "Walk-Side-Close" technique that characterizes the Modern Waltz. Because these fundamental developments of the Waltz took place in England, the Standard Waltz is sometimes known as the English Waltz. With its newer, more natural feel, the dance was soon to re-establish itself as one of the most popular ballroom social dances and to become one of the best-loved "standard" international dances.

Above: The modern Waltz has a graceful, natural feel and is now considered the most popular of standard dances.

Basic Floor Craft

While you and other dancers are dancing around the floor, you should be aware of other couples and their likely direction of travel. Knowing how to avoid problems is a great advantage to a dancer, and ways of doing this are described in the Floor Craft sections later in the book. There are, however, a few general rules worth mentioning now.

• It makes sense for more experienced dancers to give way to less experienced couples.

• If you see a potential problem, you should take action to avoid it. Usually the couples farther back in the flow of floor traffic have the best perspective.

• Never dance across the center line of the room into the oncoming flow of floor traffic.

With a little practice, the ability to avoid dancing into a problem will itself yield satisfaction and enjoyment.

Based on the techniques defined during the 1920s and cultivated through the 1930s, the Waltz has continued to develop through the 20th century, giving rise to an astonishing variety of graceful figures that can be combined in an even more astonishing variety of ways for the enjoyment of its dancers. I hope you are now about to become one of them.

On the Floor

The dance floor, whether crowded or not, is a very valuable asset and should be treated, like its users, with the utmost respect.

Always walk around the edge of the floor and never across it, especially while people are dancing. The sudden emergence of a bystander trying to dodge dancers can cause chaos on the floor and is an unnecessary hazard for dancers.

When taking to the floor, it is important to avoid causing problems to the dancers who are already there. Since men normally start a dance facing the outside of the room, it may seem quite natural for them to walk onto the floor backward while their attention is focused on their partner.

Waltz Music

Waltz music is organized with three beats to each bar of music. The Basic Waltz is also organized into sections of three steps. Each step therefore corresponds to a single beat of music. Musically, the first beat in each bar is accentuated or emphasized, and it is on this beat that you should start to dance. While the beat is giving a count of 1-2-3, you should be dancing the Walk-Side-Close movements of the Basic Waltz.

The time signature of a Waltz is 3/4 with a tempo currently recommended internationally as 30 bars per minute. This means that it takes only two seconds to dance each section of the Waltz, though this is in fact a relatively easy pace that you can really enjoy.

As this will cause a hindrance to the dancers, it is much better to approach the floor and assess the flow of floor traffic before taking up your starting position, with due consideration for the other dancers.

When leaving the floor, especially during the course of a dance, the same consideration should be shown. If you are finishing during the dance, you should dance to the edge of the floor, leave the floor at that point and walk back around the perimeter to return to your seat.

Left: Take up the starting position only when you have assessed the situation on the dance floor. Do not dance onto the floor as this may hinder other dancers.

The Dance Floor

Before you begin learning the steps, here are some basic ways of orienting yourself in the room.

• The flow of the floor traffic (the dancers) will be in an counterclockwise direction around the room.
• In the Basic Waltz, progression around the room is achieved by making a series of zigzag moves along the floor.
• The orientation of the dancers will be described in relation to the nearest wall, the center line of the floor and in terms of zigs and zags.

GOING WITH THE FLOW
Assuming that the room is rectangular, stand adjacent to any wall, making sure the wall is on the man's right and the woman's left. The man will now be in position to move forward with the flow of floor traffic and the woman to move backward. In some steps, the man will face against the flow of traffic with the wall on his left side. The overall movement of the figure being danced, however, will continue to go with the flow.

THE CENTER LINE
Still in the same position, the center line of the room will be on the man's left and the woman's right.

Right: This diagram illustrates the main ways in which the dancers orient themselves in the room. You can start to get used to this by practicing at home.

ZIGS AND ZAGS
A diagonal line, which we will call a "zig," extends from the center line to the wall parallel to it at an angle of approximately 45°. Another diagonal line, a "zag," extends from the wall to the center line at an angle of approximately 45°. In the Basic Waltz, the man moves forward along the zigs and backward along the zags in order to "tack" along the room. Conversely, the woman moves backward along the zigs and forward along the zags, opposite her partner, as they both travel with the flow. Remember that, as you dance around the room, you will encounter corners.

CORNERING
When you turn a corner, you will orient yourself using the new wall and the center line, which is always parallel to the wall you are using. The zigs and zags run along the diagonals between the new center line and the new wall, as before. The flow will, of course, flow around the corner.

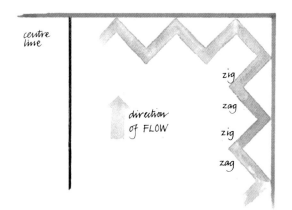

The Hold

When taking up a hold, the man takes the woman's right hand in his left hand and draws her to him. This enables him to place her slightly to his right. When in the correct position, the buttons on the man's shirt should be opposite the woman's right shoulder.

To take up the hold, the man presents his left hand as if he is a policeman stopping traffic. The woman then places the hooked middle finger of her right hand between the thumb and forefinger of the man's left hand, palm to palm. Next, the woman places her forefinger and third finger on top of her middle finger, rests her little finger on top of the others and curls her thumb around the man's thumb. The joined hands should be held just below eye level, with the hand-hold and arms firm, but not rigid. The man now places the fingertips of his left hand along the edge of the woman's right hand with the fingers pointing to the floor. In this way, the underside of both the man's left wrist and the woman's right wrist are facing the floor. When you start to dance, this will enhance stability considerably and make leading much easier.

The man cups the woman's left shoulder blade with his right hand, with the fingertips ideally placed against the woman's spine. The woman straightens the fingers of her left hand but allows the thumb to extend out in its normal position. She then places her left hand on the man's upper arm with a straight and flat wrist. It is unnecessary for her third and little finger to be resting on the man's arm. Both the man and the woman should hold their elbows slightly forward of their backs and a little away from the body. The shoulders should be relaxed, never tensed or hunched.

The man and woman should both stand upright, lifting the diaphragm to produce a good posture. The man and woman maintain lower diaphragm and upper stomach contact throughout much of the Waltz. They should hold their heads a little to the left and with their chins up. The weight of the head is such that it can have an adverse effect on balance if it is not held in the desired position. Do not look at your feet. The man's back and arms provide a "frame" in which the woman is held. A good frame is essential for good dancing and good leading.

Far left: The hold (rear view).

Left: The hold (front view).

Leading and Following

The hold and starting position often feel too rigid to a first-time dancer for fluidity of movement, but with a little practice, a good but relaxed posture and hold can be developed. This is one of the main skills that characterize a partner who is easy to dance with. The frame created by the man's arms and reinforced by his back and diaphragm should be held still and firm; that is to say, the arms should never move independently of the body. Once this is achieved, the woman will be able to feel a clear lead.

Much of the process of leading is not something that the man does actively but rather is the result of skillful and effective dancing. The best leading is that which leaves the woman no other option but to dance what the man intends without her really having to think about it. Once the woman has to work at following, the enjoyment is largely lost for her. The woman should accept the man's lead and not try to guess what he will do next, because she could commit herself too soon to a course of action that might be the wrong one.

The woman has a responsibility when she is moving forward and the man is moving backward. Since she is the one who can see where the couple is moving, she must indicate to the man if they are about to dance into a problem. She can do this by squeezing the thumb and middle finger of her left hand and then allowing the man to lead his evasive maneuver.

Right: The woman can indicate potential trouble to the man by squeezing his arm with her left hand.

Left: This position shows the frame created by the man's arms. The arms should move as one with the back and diaphragm. From this position, the man is able to lead the woman clearly.

Legs and Feet

It may seem surprising to save comments on the legs and feet until last. However, we dance with our whole bodies, and once the body is working properly, the feet and legs will often take care of themselves. Knees are very important, and you will feel more comfortable, relaxed and in control if you can keep your knees flexed at all times. Dancing, in a basic sense, is not so very different from walking, and yet it is common that someone who can walk perfectly well will feel challenged when taking a normal walk forward, simply because they are "dancing" and not walking down the street.

Try not to get too far away from your partner or worry about stepping on their feet. When the man walks forward with the right foot, with the woman positioned slightly to the man's right, his foot will go between the woman's feet. When he walks forward with the left foot he will be walking outside the woman. The same occurs when the woman is moving forward and the man is moving backward. Using this helpful technique, there is very little chance of stepping on a partner's foot, unless you create a gap between the two of you.

TAKING A STEP
When taking a step, move your foot into position and then move your body weight onto that foot.

WHICH FOOT TO START WITH
Some teachers teach the Waltz starting with the left foot for the man. Logic suggests that when we are moving forward and want to initiate a turn to the right, we do this by curving the right foot forward. This is a good move to start with because the woman will feel the curve and instinctively know that, because she is moving backward, should start moving backward with her left foot. If the man were to start with his left foot moving forward and to dance without turning, the woman would not have a clear lead.

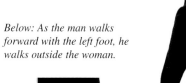

Below: As the man walks forward with the left foot, he walks outside the woman.

Above: As the man walks forward with the right foot, his foot will go between the woman's feet.

Above and right: Move your foot first, then shift your body weight into position.

The Basic Waltz

Some schools recommend dancing the Waltz in a straight line around the room. This is not incorrect, but as most dancers zigzag along the floor, the straight-line method continually cuts across the path of other dancers and causes problems for everyone. In addition, the character of the Waltz suggests a dance of elegant turns, so we will start with an internationally recognized method of dancing the Basic Waltz, which includes a degree of characteristic turning that will also make the dance more interesting and enjoyable.

GETTING ORGANIZED

The Basic Waltz described here consists of four sections of three steps to make a short routine of 12 steps. Each section has a Walk, a Side Step and a Close. Start in the hold described previously with the feet together and standing about 4 feet away from the edge of the floor to allow sufficient space to dance into. The man is ready to move forward along a zig and the woman to move backward along it.

SECTION 1

1 Man
Walk forward with the right foot, curving a little to the right (clockwise).

1 Woman
Walk back with the left foot, curving a little to the right (clockwise).

2 Man
Turn from the zig to the zag by moving sideways onto the toes of the left foot.

2 Woman
Turn from the zig to the zag by moving a small step sideways onto the toes of the right foot.

3 Man
Now, on the zag, close the right foot to the left foot and lower toe-heel onto the right foot.

3 Woman
Now, on the zag, close the left foot to the right foot and lower toe-heel onto the left foot.

SECTION 2

4 Man

Walk back along the zag onto the left foot, with no turn.

5 Man

Move sideways onto the toes of the right foot, with no turn.

6 Man

Close the left foot to the right foot and lower toe-heel onto the left foot.

4 Woman

Walk forward along the zag onto the right foot, with no turn.

5 Woman

Move sideways onto the toes of the left foot, with no turn.

6 Woman

Close the right foot to the left foot and lower toe-heel onto the right foot.

WALL

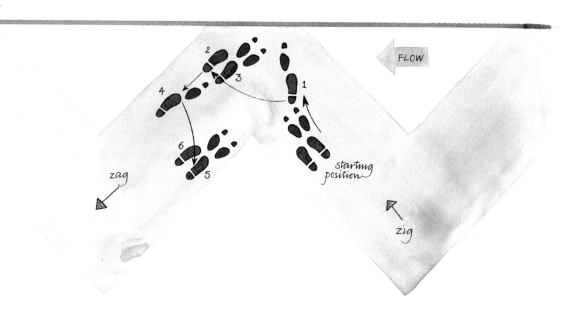

FLOW

zag

starting position

zig

SECTION 3

7 Man
Walk back with the right foot, curving a little to the left (counterclockwise).

8 Man
Turn from the zag to the zig by moving sideways onto the toes of the left foot.

9 Man
Now, on the zig, close the right foot to the left foot and lower toe-heel onto the right foot.

7 Woman
Walk forward with the left foot, curving a little to the left (counterclockwise).

8 Woman
Turn from the zag to the zig by moving sideways onto the toes of the right foot.

9 Woman
Now, on the zig, close the left foot to the right foot and lower toe-heel onto the left foot.

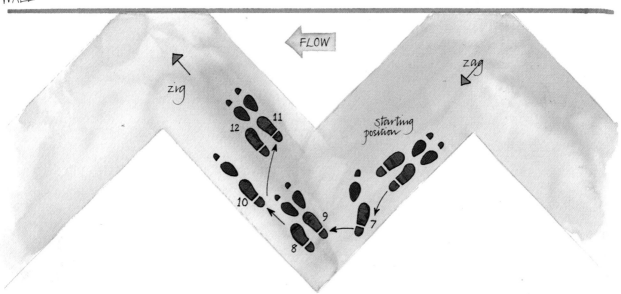

WALL

FLOW

zig

zag

starting position

12 11
10
9
8
7

SECTION 4 – *These three steps are only one of four possible examples of a Closed Change Step. A Closed Change Step is any Walk-Side-Close movement without turn. It may move forward or backward and may start with either foot.*

10 Man

Walk forward along the zig onto the left foot, with no turn.

11 Man

Move sideways onto the toes of the right foot, with no turn.

12 Man

Close the left foot to the right foot and lower toe-heel onto the left foot.

10 Woman

Walk back along the zig onto the right foot, with no turn.

11 Woman

Move sideways onto the toes of the left foot, with no turn.

12 Woman

Close the right foot to the left and lower toe-heel onto the right foot.

Notes

- Note how the sections start with alternate feet.
- The sections alternate turning moves and straight moves.
- The overall pattern of the Basic Waltz is a zigzag along the floor.
- It is essential to ensure that the second step in each section moves to the side and does not deteriorate into another walking step.
- Do not be tempted to deviate from the pattern described; accuracy is vital.
- Practice your Waltz, trying to relax and settle down to a steady rhythm. You should find that you are staying in a path about 3 feet wide.

Bad tracking?

If you find that you are "tracking" toward the center or toward the wall, you should check that you are making the same degree of turning to the right and to the left in the turning sections (Sections 1 and 3) to keep you on track.

Sway

Sway is an important feature of a nice, easy and relaxed style. When reaching with the foot, it is quite natural for the body and head to tilt or sway a little away from the reaching foot, acting as a counterbalance. If small steps are taken, sway will hardly be felt, but as you get used to dancing the Waltz and start to move more freely, it will enhance your style if you let yourself sway a little away from the reaching foot toward the closing foot.

You can now repeat the basic 12 steps from the beginning to enjoy waltzing around the room. For the moment, when you reach a corner, simply bend the dance around the corner, but make sure that you re-orient yourself as quickly as possible onto the zigs and zags of the new wall. This is best and most comfortably achieved by the man turning to the left more strongly on Step 7.

Natural Turn around a Corner

O nce you have settled down to the regular rhythm and pattern of the Basic Waltz, you will soon want to try a move which will help you turn the corner more fluently and comfortably. In standard dancing, any move which turns clockwise is referred to as a "natural" turn, no matter how unnatural it might feel at first. The Natural Turn comprises two sections of three steps. Each section follows the familiar pattern of Walk-Side-Close. Begin as for the Basic Waltz with the feet together. The man is standing on his left foot and the woman on her right foot, about 4 feet from the edge of the floor. The man is ready to move forward along a zig and the woman to move backward along it.

SECTION 1 – *This section comprises the first three steps of the Basic Waltz modified with more turning.*

1 Man
Walk forward with the right foot, curving to the right

2 Man
Continue turning and move sideways onto the toes of the left foot.

3 Man
Continue turning to end by backing into the corner, facing against the flow. Close the right foot to the left foot and lower onto the right foot. (The wall is now on your left.)

1 Woman
Walk back with the left foot, curving to the right (clockwise).

2 Woman
Continue turning and then move sideways onto the toes of the right foot (a small step).

3 Woman
Continue turning to end facing down the room with the flow. Close the left foot to the right foot and lower onto the left foot.

SECTION 2 – *Continue turning in the same direction as you cut across the corner to end on the zig at the start of the new wall.*

4 Man

Continue turning clockwise and walk back with the left foot.

5 Man

Continue turning clockwise and move sideways onto the toes of the right foot (a small step).

5 Woman

Continue turning clockwise and move sideways onto the toes of the left foot.

4 Woman

Continue turning clockwise and walk forward with the right foot.

Practical Tip – Short Steps

On Step 2 for the woman and Step 5 for the man, the dancer should take a slightly shorter step to the side to help their partner turn around them. The person who is dancing backward into the turn is the one on the "inside" of the turn and should take the shorter steps. This is a very useful tip to remember and to try to put into practice throughout the dance.

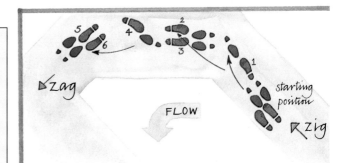

6 Man

Continue turning clockwise to end on the zig of the new wall. Close the left foot to the right foot and lower onto the left foot.

6 Woman

Continue turning clockwise to end on the zig of the new wall. Close the right foot to the left foot and lower onto the right foot.

You have now successfully turned the corner and are on a zig ready to dance along the new wall using the familiar Basic Waltz.

Rise and Fall

Rise and fall is the elevating and lowering that the dancer feels as he or she moves onto the toes of a foot and then relaxes through the knee, ankle and toes to end on a flat foot. In reality, rise and fall is a by-product of the natural swing of the Waltz that gives it the lilting flow that has ensured its continuing appeal. A good swing action is something that dedicated competitors strive to achieve over many years of tough coaching and hard practice. The social dancer can also start to enjoy the gentle rising and falling and add considerably to the feeling of the Waltz by following a few simple guidelines.

Right: A walk forward on count 1 will usually be a normal walk starting with the heel.

Left: A move to the side on count 2 will usually lift onto the toes.

Right: A close on count 3 will usually be accompanied by a lowering (toe to heel) onto the foot that has just moved to close.

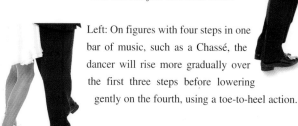

Left: On figures with four steps in one bar of music, such as a Chassé, the dancer will rise more gradually over the first three steps before lowering gently on the fourth, using a toe-to-heel action.

• Occasional exceptions to these guidelines are noted in the appropriate figure if considered relevant to the enjoyment of social dancing. There is further insight into the swing action later in the book.

Floor Craft

Your positioning on the floor and how you progress around it may be likened to driving in a flow of traffic. The skill, experience and thinking ahead necessary to negotiate the other dancers are called floor craft.

As you get used to dancing the Basic Waltz around the room and the Natural Turn around the corners, it will become apparent that there is more to floor craft than may at first be obvious. The ability to avoid problems and read the situation ahead of you are both attributes of a good dancer. This ability develops with practice but can be acquired more easily by following a few guidelines, the responsibility for which lies mainly with the man.

• It is extremely important to adhere to the given orientation in the room. If you allow yourself to wander from the prescribed path, it will be very difficult to get back to it.

• If you are following a couple around a corner, stay behind and on the wall side of the pair. By the time you reach the couple's position, they will usually have moved on.

• Avoid dancing across a corner if a couple is already in the corner. You risk being run into as the two exit the corner.

• Women, even though trying to help, should not attempt to lead the man.

All the figures described in this book have been selected not only for their attractiveness as easily enjoyable figures but also for their usefulness as floor craft figures. As your repertoire grows, so will your ability to avoid problems and then to escape from any further difficulties.

Above: Floor craft skills basically entail maneuvering around obstacles, rather like negotiating through traffic. As you become accustomed to moving around the dance floor, your style will become more relaxed and flowing.

Fitting the Basic Waltz into the Room

As you dance the Basic Waltz, you may well find that when you want to dance the Natural Turn at a corner, you are not quite in the right position; you could be either ready to dance it too early or not ready until too late. As a general rule, it is much better to dance it early, as the later option could see you disappearing off the edge of the floor. With practice, however, you will be able to gauge your progression around the room, so that you will arrive near the corner in a perfect position to dance the Natural Turn.

It is often assumed, quite wrongly, that this is achieved by increasing the length of the step. This would, in fact, make the dancing quite uncomfortable. The answer, though slightly more subtle, is no more difficult. The angle of the turns made during the Basic Waltz can be adjusted to make the dance progress more or progress less along the side of the room. A greater amount of turning will result in more progression and a lesser amount in less progression. An experienced dancer will not worry about reaching the corner in the perfect position until perhaps the last 12 steps of the Basic Waltz, in which the angles can be adjusted to fit the movement into the space available.

Be aware that less experienced dancers often try to dance an extra Basic Waltz when really they ought to have started the Natural Turn or other corner figure. This error often means that the dancer has not planned ahead sufficiently, so it is important to start thinking about the corner as soon as you have danced about two-thirds of the way along the room.

Tighter angle = Less Progression

Wider angle = More Progression

Outside Change

The most useful moves are often the simplest. The Outside Change is a great figure for using as a spacer to extend the Basic Waltz. You can dance the Outside Change immediately after dancing Section 2 of the Basic Waltz. After the Outside Change you will be able to continue by dancing your Basic Waltz again, starting with Section 1 and with the man's taking his first step forward with the right foot outside the woman, or by dancing into the Natural Turn around a Corner with the same right foot modification for the man. It can similarly be followed by the Natural Spin Turn, which is described later in the book.

1 Man
Walk back onto the left foot, still on the zag.

2 Man
Walk back onto the toes of the right foot, still on the zag.

1 Woman
Walk forward onto the right foot.

2 Woman
Walk forward onto the toes of the left foot.

3 Man

Move sideways onto the left foot, starting to move onto the zig.

Left: It is important to note that on the first step of the figure following the Outside Change, the man will find it more comfortable and natural to dance outside the woman with his right foot; that is, his right foot will move forward between himself and his partner.

WALL

1st step of next figure outside partner

zig

zag

starting position

1

3

2

FLOW

3 Woman

Move sideways onto the right foot, starting to move onto the zig.

The move is completed by continuing into the Basic Waltz or Natural Turn around a Corner.

OUTSIDE CHANGE ENDING IN PROMENADE POSITION

– This popular and extremely useful floor craft variation of the Outside Change is used to overtake slower couples ahead or just to enhance your progress around the room. It includes a new move called the Chassé (pronounced sha-say). Begin by dancing Steps 1 and 2 of the Outside Change as before. On Step 2, the man starts to move his head slightly more to the left than usual and the woman starts to move her head to the right. Then continue as follows.

3 Man

Take a small step to the side along the room by lowering onto the left foot but pointing the left foot along the zig.

3 Woman

Take a small step to the side along the room by lowering onto the right foot but pointing the right foot along the zag. Move the head over to the right.

> *In this move, the woman does not turn her body. This results in her ending in a slightly open, or Promenade Position, on Step 3.*

Promenade Position

Promenade Position is very frequently used in standard dancing. It simply means that the couple has moved into a position in which the distance between the man's left shoulder and the woman's right shoulder is greater than the distance between the man's right shoulder and woman's left. The couple is therefore slightly open on the man's left and the woman's right side. It is crucial that this very slightly open position is not exaggerated to become an almost side-by-side position. In the Promenade Position, the woman will be looking to the right and the man slightly farther to the left. When the man uses his right foot and the woman her left foot to take a step in Promenade Position, it will be taken "through the middle" between the dancers and along the same line. Such a step should be a short one to avoid distorting the top half of the body. Because of the relative position of the man and woman, the man's foot will move through ahead of the woman's.

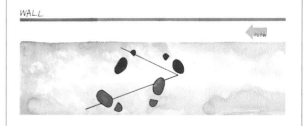

WALL

FLOW

Chassé from Promenade Position

This frequently used move has four steps. These are fitted into the standard three beats of the Waltz by dancing a special count of 1, 2 & 3, where the middle counts of 2 & share the second beat of the music. The man dances this move along a single line parallel to the wall but maintaining the zig alignment. The woman dances this move along a single line parallel to the wall but with the head and body gradually turning left to resume the normal position facing the man.

1 Man
Move the right foot forward and across yourself along the line.

2 Man
Move onto the toes of the left foot, still progressing along the same line.

& Man
Close the right foot to the left foot, still on the toes.

3 Man
Move sideways, lowering onto the left foot, along the same line, to end on the zig.

& Woman
Close the left foot to the right foot, still on the toes, completing the turn to face the man.

3 Woman
Move sideways, lowering onto the right foot, along the same line, to end on the zig.

1 Woman
Move the left foot forward and across yourself along the line, starting to turn to the left.

2 Woman
Move sideways onto the toes of the right foot, along the same line and continuing to turn left.

> *Continue into the Basic Waltz or Natural Turn around a Corner, remembering that on Step 1, the man will walk forward with the right foot outside.*

Three Walks Curving to the Right

Imagine you are on a zig ready to dance the Basic Waltz but there is another couple ahead of you. You can dance the Three Walks Curving to the Right instead. By the time you have danced this useful figure, the couple who were just ahead of you will probably have moved on, leaving your path clear.

1 Man

Walk forward onto the right foot, starting to curve to the right.

1 Woman

Walk back onto the left foot, starting to curve to the right.

Floor Craft Figures

When you first try out your Basic Waltz at a dance, you will find that one of the man's main preoccupations will be to avoid other dancers on the floor. Sometimes you will find that split-second decisions have to be made to avoid bumping into another couple. It is therefore important that the man leads the woman by making his intentions very clear. He should not and need not physically maneuver the woman if he dances his chosen move with clarity. The woman should also try to anticipate possible problems. To stop the man moving backwards into another couple, the woman should squeeze his upper right arm between her left thumb and middle finger as a warning. It is then up to the man to take the avoiding action. It is sensible to choose a figure which will avoid the problem in the simplest way. The easy moves explained here include the Hover Corté, the Whisk and the Checked Natural Turn. These, along with Three Walks Curving to the Right, will help you deal with potential traffic problems.

2 Man

Move forward onto the
toes of the left foot,
continuing to curve to
the right.

2 Woman

Move back onto the
toes of the right
foot, continuing to
curve to the right.

WALL

3

2

1

FLOW

zag

zig

starting
position

3 Man

Walk forward
and slightly
across yourself
with the right
foot, lowering
onto the right
foot outside
the woman
and continuing
to curve to the
right to end on the zag.
Turn your body a little
further to the right on
this step.

3 Woman

Walk back a small
step, lowering onto
the left foot
underneath your
body, continuing
to curve to the right
to end on the zag. Turn
your body a little further
to the right on this step.

*Continue by dancing the Outside Change with an
important modification. On Step 1, maintain the turned
body position of the end of the Three Walks Curving to
the Right. The woman takes her first step of the Outside
Change outside the man, that is, between herself and
her partner, and will start to turn a little to the left to
move in line with the man as she continues into Step 2.*

Hover Corté

The Hover Corté (pronounced kor-tay) is a standard figure in the Waltz and can be danced after Step 6 of the Basic Waltz, especially if the way ahead is not clear. Start on a zag, having danced Section 2 of the Basic Waltz. The man is standing on his left foot and the woman on her right. Both have their feet together.

1 Man
Walk back onto the right foot, curving a little to the left (counterclockwise).

1 Woman
Walk forward onto the left foot, curving a little to the left (counterclockwise).

2 Man
Move sideways onto the toes of the left foot, turning onto the zig.

2 Woman
Turn from the zag to the zig by moving sideways onto the toes of the right foot, allowing the left foot to touch the right foot underneath the body.

3 Man
On the zig, lower your body weight sideways onto the right foot.

3 Woman
On the zig, lower your body weight sideways onto the left foot.

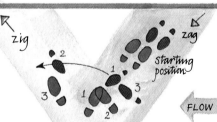

Continue with Section 2 of the Basic Waltz. Dance this without any turning so that you remain on the zig. The woman will take Step 1 forward and across herself and outside the man with the right foot. Now start the Basic Waltz from the beginning.

Whisk

The Whisk is a popular and standard move in the Waltz. A good place to dance the Whisk is after Step 9 (Section 3) of the Basic Waltz. Because the Whisk temporarily halts your progress around the room, it is a good delaying move if another couple is in the path ahead. The couple is on a zig with feet together. The man is standing on his right foot and the woman on her left.

1 Man
Walk forward onto the left foot on the zig.

1 Woman
Walk back onto the right foot on the zig.

2 Man
Move sideways against the flow onto the toes of the right foot, still on the zig.

2 Woman
Move sideways against the flow onto the toes of the left foot, turning from the zig to the zag.

3 Man
Lower onto the left foot, crossing it behind the right foot underneath your body and turning your body very slightly to the right.

3 Woman
Lower onto the right foot, crossing it behind the left foot underneath your body.

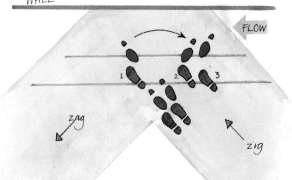

WALL

FLOW

zag

zig

> You are now in a Promenade Position with the woman having opened her right side. Continue with the Chassé from Promenade Position, which you danced previously as part of the Outside Change and Chassé from Promenade Position.

Checked Natural Turn with Reverse Pivot

If you are dancing into the Natural Turn around a Corner and you find that the corner is congested with floor traffic immediately ahead of you, you can check the movement into the turn and pivot to the left out of trouble. Start as for the Natural Turn around a Corner.

1 Man
Walk forward onto the right foot, starting to turn to the right.

1 Woman
Walk back onto the left foot, starting to turn to the right.

2 Man
Move forward onto the toes of the left foot, turning more strongly to the right but keeping your head looking along the zig. Sway a little to the left.

2 Woman
Move back onto the toes of the right foot, turning more strongly to the right. Sway a little to the right and allow your head to move over to the right.

3 Man
Curve back, lowering onto the right foot and turning strongly to the left while keeping the left foot in front of the right foot, knees together, to end on the zig of the new wall, or to be ready to move toward the center line of the room along the zag.

3 Woman
Move forward, lowering onto the left foot and turning strongly to the left with your knees together. Allow your head to move to the left to resume its normal position. End on the zig of the new wall.

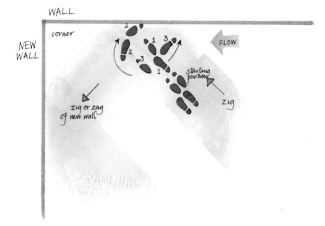

Having negotiated the corner, you can continue to dance into Steps 10–12 (Section 4) of the Basic Waltz or into the Whisk.

Floor Craft Options – A Summary

You now have a number of options to help you cope with floor traffic conditions at each stage of the Basic Waltz and at the corner, if you find the way ahead blocked.

As you practice, you will find that you will gradually be able to improve your response time to the floor conditions ahead and will increasingly be able to avoid problems by reading the floor. Of course, you don't have to wait until there is a problem to be avoided before you dance these options. You can dance them to hone your floor craft skills or just to enjoy them as figures in themselves. Practice not only makes perfect, it makes possible. When you are dancing your repertoire of moves with little effort, it is time to try something a little more challenging.

After Section 1:
Outside Change, or Outside Change ending in Promenade Position and Chassé from Promenade Position.

After Section 2:
Hover Corté.

After Section 3:
Whisk and Chassé from Promenade Position.

After Section 4:
Three Walks Curving to the Right and Outside Change.

Natural Spin Turn

While it is not a basic figure, the Natural Spin Turn has become the international standard method of turning a corner in the Waltz. The figure starts in the same place as the Natural Turn around a Corner. Think of the Natural Spin Turn as having a total of six steps. You have encountered three of them earlier so, with a little patience, you will soon be able to master this simplified version of the Natural Spin Turn. Start by dancing Steps 1–3 of the Natural Turn around a Corner. The man is facing against the flow with his feet together and standing on his right foot. The woman is facing with the flow with her feet together and standing on her left foot.

4 Man

Move back onto the left foot, staying down and turning the left foot inward to make a strong turn to the right. Keep your knees together. (This will feel awkward but only because you are dancing it step-by-step. At normal speed, the move will flow much more comfortably.)

4 Woman

Move forward onto the right foot, staying down and turning strongly to the right to end on the zig of the new wall. Keep your knees together.

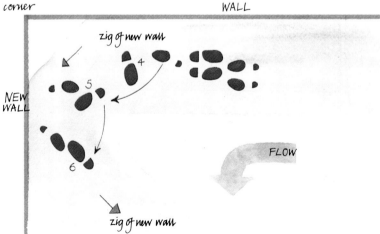

5 Man

Walk forward between the woman's feet onto the right foot on the zig of the new wall. Lift up onto the toes of the right foot and continue turning to the right on the toes of the right foot, keeping the left foot behind.

Floor Craft Tip

If you find the corner blocked as you start the Natural Spin Turn, you can stop the figure by dancing the Checked Natural Turn with Reverse Pivot described earlier.

6 Man

Relax back onto the left foot away from the corner, having turned onto the zag of the new wall.

5 Woman

Move back onto the toes of the left foot on the zig of the new wall, continuing to turn to the right. Bring your right foot back out of the way to touch your left foot.

6 Woman

Move forward, lowering onto the right foot on the zag of the new wall.

Style Tip

Some men find it helpful to think of Steps 4–6 as a rock back, a rock forward lifting and a rock back while remembering, of course, to turn. It is a common error for the man to make Step 5 a side step but this must be avoided. It is important for the man to keep his head to the left throughout the figure.

Note that the feet do not close. Continue by dancing straight into Section 3 of the Basic Waltz.

Hover Telemark

The Hover Telemark is a classic figure that is not only extremely useful but also has a superb look and feel and is not difficult to lead. The description of the moves needs to be carefully followed before success will be achieved. Do not confuse the name of this move with the Hover Corté described earlier. Dance this figure after Section 3 of the Basic Waltz. You will now be on a zig with your feet together. The man is standing on his right foot and the woman on her left.

1 Man
Walk forward onto the left foot along the zig but turning your body to the left so that you are almost walking across yourself. Relax the knees and look along the zig.

1 Woman
Walk backward onto the right foot along the zig but turning your body to the left so that you are almost walking across yourself. Relax the knees and turn your head well to the left as you feel the clear lead of this figure.

2 Man
Move forward along the zig onto the toes of the right foot, turning your body to the right so that it comes square with the feet.

2 Woman
Move back along the zig onto the toes of the left foot, turning your body to the right so that it comes square with the feet. Move your head gradually over to the right to end facing the man.

3 Man
Take a small step to the side along the room by lowering onto the left foot and pointing it along the zig in a Promenade Position.

3 Woman
Take a small step to the side along the room by lowering onto the right foot and pointing it along the zag. Move your head over to the right to finish in a Promenade Position.

Continue with the Chassé from Promenade Position.

Open Telemark Group

Now that you have had some practice at combining the figures you have learned and have become familiar with various features of the Waltz, including the Promenade Position, you will certainly want to try a new combination as this move is introduced. Take care and consider the other dancers, as this combination moves you across the flow towards the center line of the room. First, though, you will need to position yourself ready to dance the Open Telemark.

SECTION 1 – *Dance the Natural Spin Turn as you would at a corner and using the same amount of turning, but this time dance it along the side of the room. When you have danced a complete 360° turn, you will end on the zig against the flow.*

SECTION 2 – *Dance Section 3 of the Basic Waltz to end facing towards the center line of the room but on the zag. You will have turned 90° to the left. You are now ready to experience the elegance of the Open Telemark.*

1 Man

Walk forward onto the left foot along the zag toward the center line, starting to turn to the left.

2 Man

Move forward onto the toes of the right foot, still along the zag toward the center line and continuing to turn to the left. End with the right foot to the side, backing the zig.

3 Man

Continue turning on the right foot and take a small step to the side, lowering onto the left foot and pointing it along the zig in Promenade Position.

1 Woman

Walk back onto the right foot along the zag toward the center line, starting to turn to the left.

2 Woman

Close the left foot to the right foot with the left heel in contact with the floor. Continue turning to the left on the heel of the right foot and move your head gradually over to the right as you rise onto the toes of the left foot.

3 Woman

Continue turning on the left foot and take a small step to the side, lowering onto the right foot and pointing it along the room in Promenade Position. Your head is now to the right.

Continue with the Chassé from Promenade Position.

Hesitation Change

You have already seen how figures can be modified to produce variations and how the same moves can be danced in a different orientation or alignment. Here is a variation of the Natural Turn which you can use as an entry into the Open Telemark. Dance Steps 1–3 of the Natural Turn. End with your feet together, the man standing on his right foot facing with the flow and the woman on her left foot. Steps 4–5 of this figure are devised as a continuous, fluid movement for the man.

4 Man

Walk back onto the left foot, continuing to turn to the right and releasing the right toes from the floor but keeping the right heel in contact with the floor.

5 Man

Pull the right foot back with the heel in contact with the floor, then slide the foot around to end beside the left foot with the feet apart, continuing the turn to end standing on the right foot. End facing along the zag toward the center line.

6 Man

Slide the left foot to close to the right foot but remain standing on the right foot.

4 Woman

Walk forward onto the right foot, continuing to turn to the right.

5 Woman

Move sideways onto the left foot, staying down with flexed knees and continuing to turn. End on the zag, backing the center line.

6 Woman

Slide the right foot to close to the left foot but remain standing on the left foot.

Continue with the Open Telemark, the Progressive Chassé to the Right or the Reverse Turn.

Progressive Chassé to the Right

This is a very simple figure with which you can easily progress along the room or dance as an alternative to the Open Telemark if the way ahead is blocked or congested. As with the previous chassé figure, this move has four steps and is danced to a count of 1, 2 & 3. The move starts with the man facing along the zag toward the center line of the room. This position can be reached by dancing either the entry group to the Open Telemark or the Hesitation Change. A more spectacular alternative would be to dance the Checked Natural Turn with Reverse Pivot.

1 Man
Walk forward onto the left foot, starting to turn to the left. You have now stepped onto an imaginary line parallel to the wall.

2 Man
Move sideways along the line onto the toes of the right foot and continue turning slightly to the left to end with your back square to the wall.

& Man
Close the left foot to the right foot, still on the toes, and continue to turn to the left to end backing along the zig.

1 Woman
Walk back onto the right foot, starting to turn to the left. You have now stepped onto an imaginary line parallel to the wall.

2 Woman
Move sideways along the line onto the toes of the left foot and continue turning slightly to the left to point the left foot along the zig.

& Woman
Close the right foot to the left foot, still on the toes, and continue to turn to the left to end facing along the zig.

3 Man
Move sideways, still along the line, lowering onto the right foot.

3 Woman
Move sideways, still along the line, lowering onto the left foot.

Continue with the Outside Change, but with the following modifications to allow you to cope with the added turn necessary to end ready to dance on the zig.

The Exit

1 Man
Walk back along the line, under the body and onto the left foot, turning to the left to face against the flow.

2 Man
Walk back along the line onto the toes of the right foot, bringing the woman in line with you and continuing to turn to the left.

3 Man
Move sideways along the line, lowering onto the left foot to end on the zig.

1 Woman
Take a small step forward with the right foot, along the line and outside the man, starting to turn to the left to face along the room.

2 Woman
Walk forward along the line onto the toes of the left foot, turning to the left to end in line with the man.

3 Woman
Move sideways onto the right foot, continuing to turn to end backing along the zig.

The options now open to you include starting the Basic Waltz, the Three Walks Curving to the Right, the Natural Turn around a Corner, the Natural Spin Turn or the Hesitation Change. Whichever move the man chooses, he will take the first step outside the woman with his right foot.

Hairpin from Promenade Position

The Outside Change, the Whisk, the Hover Telemark and the Open Telemark can or do all end in Promenade Position and would normally be followed by the Chassé from Promenade Position. However, as the route ahead may sometimes be blocked, it is useful to have an alternative course available to you. Here is a superb figure which always looks more difficult than it is, giving professional polish to the Waltz of even moderate dancers. Start by dancing any of the figures listed above, ending in Promenade Position.

1 Man
Move the right foot forward and across yourself along the line.

1 Woman
Move the left foot forward and across yourself along the line.

Style Tip
The man dances Steps 1–2 along a single line parallel to the wall but maintaining the zig alignment. The woman dances Steps 1–2 along a single line parallel to the wall.

2 Man
Move onto the toes of the left foot, pointing them along the zig. Close the woman to your right side by turning your body slightly to the left.

2 Woman
Move sideways onto the toes of the right foot, along the same line but turning strongly to the left to close your right side to the man. Your head resumes its normal left position.

3 Man
On the left foot, sway and turn strongly to the right onto the zag. Take a small step forward, lowering onto the right foot outside the woman. Turn your body a little farther to the right as you take this step and move your head to the right to look at the woman. Note that the body turn occurs before the step.

3 Woman
Take a small step back, under your body, lowering onto the left foot and turning strongly to the right to end on the zag. Turn your body a little farther to the right as you take this step.

Note the strong sway to the right for the man and to the left for the woman on Step 3. Continue into the Outside Change.

Hairpin from Step 6 of the Basic Waltz

The Hairpin does not have to be danced from the Promenade Position. It can also be started from Step 6 of the Basic Waltz, in which case it is modified as follows. Use it in any situation where the way ahead is blocked and you wish to delay your progress around the room.

1 Man
Walk back onto the right foot along the zag.

1 Woman
Walk forward onto the left foot along the zag.

2 Man
Move sideways onto the toes of the left foot.

2 Woman
Take a small step sideways onto the toes of the right foot.

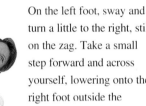

3 Man
On the left foot, sway and turn a little to the right, still on the zag. Take a small step forward and across yourself, lowering onto the right foot outside the woman. Turn your body a little farther to the right as you take this step and move your head to the right to look at the woman.

3 Woman
Take a small step back under your body, lowering onto the left foot and turning a little to the right. Turn your body a little farther to the right as you take this step.

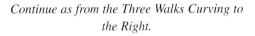

Continue as from the Three Walks Curving to the Right.

Wing

The Wing is an elegant figure that can be used to link a Promenade Position with the Progressive Chassé to the Right. A favorite place to dance the Wing is after the Whisk, but it can also be danced after the Outside Change ending in Promenade Position, the Hover Telemark or the Open Telemark. In this figure, the man halts his forward progress to lead the woman to dance three walks around him to finish on his left side – the opposite side of normal. Start after dancing any of the figures listed above, ending in Promenade Position.

1 Man

Walk forward and across yourself onto the right foot, starting to turn to the left.

1 Woman

Walk forward onto the left foot, starting to walk around the man.

Style Tip

To enhance the woman's appearance, she should sway to the left on Steps 2 and 3 and turn her hips towards the man. The couple should try to maintain contact during Steps 2 and 3.

2 Man

Leaving the right foot in place, continue to swivel to the left on the right foot while drawing the left foot towards the right foot. Leave the left foot in contact with the floor, without putting any weight on it.

2 Woman

Walk forward onto the toes of the right foot, continuing to walk around the man.

3 Man

On the right foot, complete a 90° turn, swivelling to the left. Close the left foot to the right foot but remain standing on the right foot. You are now on a zag.

3 Woman

Lowering onto the left foot, walk forward between yourself and the man's left side. You are now on a zag.

Continue with the man stepping forward with his left foot outside the woman's left side on the first step of the Progressive Chassé to the Right.

Reverse Turn

If you have successfully accomplished all the figures up to this point, it is time to venture into the domain of the more experienced dancer, away from the wall and toward the center line of the room, with this relatively easy figure. The name of the move simply indicates that the turn will be made to the left. The entry is the same as for the Open Telemark Group or you can simply dance the Hesitation Change. Start with the man on a zag ready to move forward toward the center line. With feet together, the man is standing on his right foot and the woman on her left.

1 Man
Walk forward with the left foot, curving to the left.

2 Man
Continuing to turn to the left, move sideways onto the toes of the right foot.

3 Man
Continuing to turn to the left to end facing against the flow, close the left foot to the right foot and lower onto the left foot.

1 Woman
Walk back with the right foot, curving to the left.

2 Woman
Continuing to turn to the left, move sideways onto the toes of the left foot.

3 Woman
Continuing to turn to the left to end facing with the flow, close the right foot to the left and lower onto the right foot.

4 Man

Continuing to turn to the left, walk back onto the right foot.

4 Woman

Continuing to turn to the left, walk forward onto the left foot.

5 Man

Continuing to turn to the left, move sideways onto the toes of the left foot.

5 Woman

Continuing to turn to the left, move sideways onto the toes of the right foot.

6 Man

Continuing to turn to the left to end on the zig, close the right foot to the left foot and lower onto the right foot.

6 Woman

Continuing to turn to the left to end on the zig, close the left foot to the right foot and lower onto the left foot.

Continue with Section 4 of the Basic Waltz, the Whisk or the Hover Telemark.

Three Walks Curving to the Left

To give you added flexibility in your choice of moves, you may occasionally like to substitute Three Walks Curving to the Left for steps 1–3 of the Reverse Turn. Be careful not to dance the figure against the flow. Start in the same position as for the Reverse Turn.

1 Man
Walk forward with the left foot, curving to the left.

1 Woman
Walk back with the right foot, curving to the left.

2 Man
Walk forward onto the toes of the right foot, still curving and swaying to the left.

2 Woman
Walk back onto the toes of the left foot, still curving and swaying to the left.

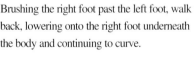

3 Man
Brushing the left foot past the right foot, walk forward, lowering onto the left foot and continuing to curve.

3 Woman
Brushing the right foot past the left foot, walk back, lowering onto the right foot underneath the body and continuing to curve.

The figure ends with the man facing against the flow and the woman facing with the flow. Continue into either the Progressive Chassé to the Left or simply Steps 4–6 of the Reverse Turn. A more advanced and dynamic exit uses the Hairpin (as danced after Step 6 of the Basic Waltz), ending with the man backing the zig. This move could then be followed by any of the moves which follow the Progressive Chassé to the Right.

Reverse Turn Chassé

For the technically minded, this figure is properly called 1–3 Reverse Turn with a Progressive Chassé to the Left. As this rather lengthy title suggests, you will start with the first three steps of the Reverse Turn. The man has now lowered onto his left foot with his feet together and is facing against the flow. The woman has lowered onto her right foot with feet together and is facing with the flow. The dancers will continue with a Chassé movement using the characteristic 1, 2 & 3 count. The Chassé is danced as usual along an imaginary line parallel to the wall.

PROGRESSIVE CHASSÉ TO THE LEFT

4 Man
Walk back onto the right foot, starting to turn to the left.

5 Man
Continuing to turn to the left, move sideways onto the toes of the left foot.

& Man
Continuing to turn to the left, close the toes of the right foot to the toes of the left foot.

4 Woman
Walk forward onto the left foot, starting to turn to the left.

5 Woman
Continuing to turn to the left, move sideways onto the toes of the right foot.

& Woman
Continuing to turn to the left, close the toes of the left foot to the toes of the right foot.

6 Man

Continuing to turn to the left to end on the zig, move sideways, lowering onto the left foot.

6 Woman

Continuing to turn to the left to end on the zig, move sideways, lowering onto the right foot.

Settling Down

When first embarking on the adventure of attending a social dance, most people who regard themselves as beginners almost always feel a little intimidated. Everyone else seems to be so expert, and when the time comes to take the floor, you may feel that everyone is looking at you with a critical eye. It is important to realize that, while such feelings are perfectly normal, a newcomer should try to keep things in perspective. More experienced or advanced dancers may seem to be more expert, but this illusion is often due more to their relaxed confidence than their real ability as dancers. Having a greater repertoire of figures or having danced for longer will not necessarily make someone a better dancer. A new dancer frequently feels that all eyes are watching and waiting for that inevitable mistake. In fact, most people are much more interested in their own dancing than that of others. Of course, if there is a particular couple that is quietly exhibiting a nice style, then it may attract the admiring attention of spectators. However, while everyone may enjoy seeing an expert couple, resentment will quickly follow if the dancers are perceived to be "showing off." It is grossly impolite and inappropriate to dance in a "competitive" or ostentatious style at a social dance. A less experienced couple will not attract critical attention. The trick for the newcomer is just to relax, get out there and enjoy the dance. And if you do make a mistake – does it really matter? You won't have been the first, and you certainly won't be the last. Laugh it off and start again.

Continue with the man stepping forward outside the woman on the first step of the Basic Waltz, the Natural Turn, the Natural Spin Turn, the Three Walks Curving to the Right or the Hesitation Change.

Open Impetus Turn

This sounds quite a dramatic turn but don't let that put you off learning this superb figure, which you can enjoy incorporating into your program. There is a lot to do on Step 2, but it is only a sequence of events that can easily be mastered with a little patience. Stay relaxed and don't try to overdo it. Start by dancing the first three steps of the Natural Turn. With feet together, the man is now standing on his right foot facing against the flow and the woman is standing on her left foot facing with the flow.

1 Man
Take a small step back onto the left foot, starting to turn to the right.

1 Woman
Walk forward onto the right foot, starting to turn to the right.

2 Man
Close the right foot to the left foot by staying down and pulling the heel of the right foot strongly to close.

2 Woman
Begin the move with your head over to the left. Walk forward past the man onto the toes of the left foot and turn to the right so that your feet end side-by-side but apart and you are on a zag, backing the center line.

2 Man (Cont.)

On the left foot, continue turning to the right, aided by the impetus of the right foot closing back and by swaying and looking to the right, to end facing along the zag towards the center line. Lift onto the toes of the right foot, feet still together, returning your head to its normal position.

3 Man

On the toes of the right foot, continue turning a little to face down the room with the flow. Take a small step onto the toes of the left foot along the zag towards the center line, then lower onto the left foot in a Promenade Position, looking to the left.

3 Woman

Continuing to turn on the left foot, take a small step onto the toes of the right foot along the zag towards the center line, then lower onto the right foot in a Promenade Position, looking to the right.

Continue with the Wing and the
Progressive Chassé to the Right, the Hover from
Promenade Position or the Weave.

2 Woman (Cont.)

Sway a little to the left to match the man. Allow the right foot to neutralize under your body by touching it to the left foot.

Hover from Promenade Position

It is always good practice and style to have a floor craft figure up your sleeve that you can dance if the way ahead is blocked or congested. This one can be danced in such circumstances after the Open Impetus Turn. Steps 2 and 3 are similar to the Hover Corté but the entry is from a Promenade Position, moving along the zag towards the center line, and there is also a turn from the zag to the zig.

1 Man
Walk forward and across yourself onto the right foot, along the zag and in Promenade Position.

1 Woman
Walk forward and across yourself onto the left foot, along the zag and in Promenade Position.

2 Man
Take a small step forward onto the toes of the left foot, turning to the left to face along the zag. Lead the "hover" by swaying to the right on this step.

2 Woman
Walk forward onto the toes of the right foot, turning to the left to end facing the man with your feet side-by-side but apart. Sway to the left and turn your head to the left.

3 Man
On the toes of the left foot, continue turning to the left and move sideways, lowering onto the right foot to end backing along the zig.

3 Woman
On the toes of the right foot, continue turning to the left and move sideways, lowering onto the left foot to face along the zig.

Continue with one of the figures suggested for following the Progressive Chassé to the Right. You may even dance into the Open Impetus Turn from this position. Remember that the next step for the woman will be a forward walk with her right foot outside the man.

Weave

This six-step figure has become one of the international standard moves in the Waltz and this version is designed to be danced after the Open Impetus Turn. Unusually for the Waltz, the dancers do not close their feet during the Weave. After the Open Impetus Turn, the dancers will have just moved onto the zag in Promenade Position. The man is standing on his left foot and the woman on her right foot.

1 Man
Walk forward and across yourself along the zag onto the right foot, starting to turn to the left.

2 Man
Take a small step forward along the zag onto the toes of the left foot between the woman's feet, continuing to turn to the left.

3 Man
Move sideways and a little back, lowering onto the right foot and continuing to turn to the left to end facing against the flow.

1 Woman
Walk forward and across yourself along the zag onto the left foot, starting to turn to the left.

2 Woman
Move sideways onto the toes of the right foot, turning to the left to face the man and returning your head to its normal position to the left.

3 Woman
Move sideways and a little forward, lowering onto the left foot and continuing to turn to the left to end facing with the flow.

4 Man

Walk back onto the left foot under your body, continuing to turn to the left.

5 Man

Walk back onto the toes of the right foot, continuing to turn to the left.

6 Man

Move sideways, lowering onto the left foot to end with the left foot on the zig and your body facing the wall.

4 Woman

Walk forward and slightly across yourself onto the right foot outside the man's right side.

5 Woman

Walk forward onto the toes of the left foot, moving in line with the man and starting again to turn to the left.

6 Woman

Move sideways, lowering onto the right foot to end backing the wall.

Continue with the Basic Waltz, the Natural Turn, the Hesitation Change, the Natural Spin Turn or the Three Walks Curving to the Right. The man will take the first step of whichever figure you choose by walking forward with his right foot outside the woman.

Promenade Ending to the Weave

One of the attractions of the Weave is its flexibility. Having danced Steps 1–3 of the Weave, you have the choice of ending the move as described above or of substituting an ending which will leave you in Promenade Position and able to travel more directly along the room if desired. The feeling of the Promenade Ending to the Weave is very similar to dancing an Outside Change ending in Promenade Position. Start by dancing Steps 1–3 of the Weave.

4 Man
Walk back onto the left foot under your body, continuing to turn to the left.

4 Woman
Walk forward and slightly across yourself onto the right foot outside the man's right side.

5 Man
Walk back onto the toes of the right foot, continuing to turn to the left.

5 Woman
Walk forward onto the toes of the left foot, moving in line with the man and starting again to turn to the left.

6 Man
Take a small step sideways, lowering onto the left foot to end with the left foot on the zig. With a slight press of the right hand, lead the woman into Promenade Position.

6 Woman
Move forward, lowering onto the right foot pointing along the zag and turning your head to the right to end in Promenade Position.

You can now move fluently into a Chassé from Promenade Position. If the hazard ahead looks unlikely to clear quickly, the Hairpin from Promenade Position will take you toward the wall. Note that the Weave cannot be danced from this position in the room.

Oversway

This classic figure has a number of forms and styles; in this version, the couple come to a temporary halt as the man leads the woman into a turn enhanced by a slightly exaggerated sway. Since the turn is done in place, this move is also useful as a very classy floor craft figure. Start by dancing Steps 1–3 of the Reverse Turn or the Three Walks Curving to the Left. The man is now facing against the flow, standing on his left foot with feet together. The woman is facing with the flow, standing on her right foot with feet together. The Oversway is danced along a line parallel to the wall.

1 Man
Walk back along the line onto the right foot.

1 Woman
Walk forward onto the left foot.

2 Man
Walk back along the line onto the left foot, relaxing the knee then, on the left foot, start to swivel to the left, with a slight sway to the left, and lead the woman as if you are moving her into Promenade Position.

2 Woman
Walk forward onto the ball of the right foot as if ready to pass the man, leading with your right side, and flex the right knee, leaving the left foot extended behind. On the right foot, swivel to the left with a slight sway to the right. End with your head to the right.

3 Man
Still on the left foot, with the knee flexed and increasing the sway to the left slightly, continue to swivel to the left to end facing the wall with the right foot extended to the side but without any weight on it.

3 Woman
Still on the right foot, with the knee flexed and increasing the sway to the right slightly, continue to swivel to the left to end backing the wall with the left foot extended to the side but without any weight on it.

4 Man

Still on the left foot with the left knee flexed and the right foot extended to the side, continue to swivel onto the zig, changing the sway from left to right and bringing your left side back a little and pushing forward through the hips.

5 Man

Close the right foot to the left foot, then lift onto the toes of the right foot and neutralize the sway, leading the woman into Promenade Position.

6 Man

Take a small step sideways along the room, lowering onto the left foot in Promenade Position.

4 Woman

Still on the right foot with the knee flexed and the left foot extended to the side, continue to swivel onto the zig, changing the sway from right to left and allowing your head to return to the left. The sway to the left should be slightly exaggerated by turning the body a little more to the left.

5 Woman

Close the left foot to the right foot, then lift onto the toes of the left foot and neutralize the sway as you return your head to the right to end in Promenade Position.

6 Woman

Take a small step sideways along the room, lowering onto the right foot in Promenade Position.

The best exit is now a Chassé from Promenade Position, though any of the exits suggested for the Promenade Ending to the Weave can be selected.

Swing

A good swing epitomizes the action used by expert dancers of the Waltz. While in the early stages of getting to grips with the Waltz, you will not have much time to think about developing a good action but sooner or later you will want to enhance your enjoyment and improve your style with a little bit of swing. If you were to suspend a pendulum from the ceiling, then pull it back and release it to fall by the force of gravity, it would travel in an arc along a straight line. You can begin to use such a natural swing in your Waltz. In most of the figures in standard dancing, swing acts on alternate sides of the body in each bar of music or set of three steps. Swing can be applied to any figure and here the Natural Turn is used as an example.

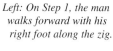

Left: On Step 1, the man walks forward with his right foot along the zig.

Left: As the man turns to the right on Step 2, swing will act on his left side, causing him to rise and helping to propel his left side towards the wall faster than his right side, which has become the center of the turn.

Below: On Step 3, the swing naturally continues upwards, taking the man's left side with it and causing him to turn and continue rising with the swing's momentum. When the dancer is turning, the swing action will also cause him or her to incline the body towards the center of the turn – this inclination is called "sway."

Left: Since swing occurs in a straight line, the feet also use that straight line. Steps 1–3 of the Natural Turn are all taken on the same line (in this example, on the zig), irrespective of the turn and where the feet happen to be facing. On Steps 4–6, each step will be taken on the same floorboard or line parallel with the wall, while the swing will act on the man's right side.

Style Tip

When dancing with a swing action, Step 2, which is usually a side step, carries the powerful swing momentum and will therefore be longer than Steps 1 or 3.

Swing is responsible for maintaining a proportional amount of turn, alignment, rise and fall, footwork, sway and length of step in many Waltz figures. Swing also leads to a less energetic and more economical way of moving. It is an important ingredient of good dancing and one that your local coach or dance school can help you develop further.

Figures and Combinations

The following tables give suggestions for combining the figures you have learned to create your own routines.

Figures starting with the man moving the right foot forward toward the wall on a zig.

1 Section 1 of the Basic Waltz
2 Closed Change Step
3 Natural Turn
4 Natural Spin Turn
5 Three Walks Curving to the Right
6 Checked Natural with Reverse Pivot
7 Hesitation Change
8 Open Impetus Turn starting with Steps 1–3 of the Natural Turn

Figures starting with the man moving the left foot back away from the wall on a zag.

1 Section 2 of the Basic Waltz (a Closed Change Step)
2 Outside Change

Figures starting with the man moving the right foot back away from the wall on a zag.

1 Section 3 of the Basic Waltz
2 Closed Change Step
3 Hover Corté
4 Hairpin
5 Steps 4–6 of the Reverse Turn ending to face with the flow and continuing into the Progressive Chassé to the Right

Figures starting with the man moving the left foot forward toward the wall on a zig.

1 Closed Change Step (Section 4 of the Basic Waltz)
2 Whisk
3 Hover Telemark

Figures starting with the man moving the left foot forward toward the center line on a zag.

1 Reverse Turn
2 Closed Change Step
3 Three Walks Curving to the Left
4 Reverse Turn Chassé
5 Open Telemark
6 Progressive Chassé to the Right
7 Oversway starting with Steps 1–3 of the Reverse Turn or Three Walks Curving to the Left

Figures starting from Promenade Position and moving along the room.

1 Chassé from Promenade Position
2 Wing followed by the Progressive Chassé to the Right
3 Hairpin from Promenade Position

Figures starting from Promenade Position and moving towards the center line on a zag.

1 Weave
2 Hover from Promenade Position
3 Wing followed by the Progressive Chassé to the Right

PRECEDING AND FOLLOWING FIGURES

Section 1 of the Basic Waltz

Preceding Figures:
Section 4 of the Basic Waltz
Outside Change
Natural Turn around a Corner
Chassé from Promenade Position
Reverse Turn Chassé
Weave

Following Figures:
Section 2 of the Basic Waltz
Outside Change
Outside Change ending in Promenade Position

Section 2 of the Basic Waltz

Preceding Figures:
Section 1 of the Basic Waltz
Three Walks Curving to the Right (for the woman, Step 1 of
    Section 2 of the Basic Waltz would be taken outside the man)

Following Figures:
Section 3 of the Basic Waltz
Hover Corté
Section 2 of the Open Telemark Group
Hairpin

Section 3 of the Basic Waltz

Preceding Figures:
Section 2 of the Basic Waltz
Natural Spin Turn

Following Figures:
Section 4 of the Basic Waltz
Whisk
Hover Telemark

Section 4 of the Basic Waltz

Preceding Figures:
Section 3 of the Basic Waltz
Reverse Turn
Hesitation Change around a Corner

Following Figures:
Section 1 of the Basic Waltz
Natural Turn around a Corner
Natural Spin Turn
Checked Natural with Reverse Pivot
Three Walks Curving to the Right
Hesitation Change
Steps 1–3 of the Natural Turn
    followed by the Open Impetus Turn

Natural Turn around a Corner

Preceding Figures:
Section 4 of the Basic Waltz
Outside Change
Chassé from Promenade
    Position
Reverse Turn Chassé
Weave

Following Figures:
Section 1 of the Basic Waltz
Natural Turn around a Corner
Natural Spin Turn
Three Walks Curving to the Right
Checked Natural with Reverse Pivot
Hesitation Change
Steps 1–3 of the Natural Turn
    followed by the Open
    Impetus Turn

Outside Change

Preceding Figures:
Section 1 of the Basic Waltz
Three Walks Curving to the Right
Progressive Chassé to the Right
Hairpin

Precedes (if ended in a normal position):
Section 1 of the Basic Waltz
Natural Turn around a Corner
Natural Spin Turn
Three Walks Curving to the Right
Checked Natural with Reverse Pivot
Hesitation Change
Steps 1–3 of the Natural Turn followed by the
    Open Impetus Turn

Precedes (if ended in Promenade Position):
Chassé from Promenade Position
Hairpin from Promenade Position
Wing followed by the Progressive Chassé to
    the Right

Chassé from Promenade Position

Preceding Figures:
Outside Change ending in Promenade Position
Whisk
Hover Telemark
Weave ending in Promenade Position
Open Impetus Turn following the Progressive Chassé to the Right

Following Figures:
Section 1 of the Basic Waltz
Natural Turn around a Corner
Natural Spin Turn
Three Walks Curving to the Right
Checked Natural with Reverse Pivot
Hesitation Change
Steps 1–3 of the Natural Turn followed by the Open Impetus Turn

Three Walks Curving to the Right

Preceding Figures:
Section 4 of the Basic Waltz
Outside Change
Natural Turn around a Corner
Chassé from Promenade Position
Reverse Turn Chassé
Weave

Following Figures:
Section 2 of the Basic Waltz
Outside Change
Outside Change ending in Promenade
    Position
Open Impetus Turn (overturned)

**(N.B. The woman will start outside the man on Step 1 of
the above figures.)**

Hover Corté

Preceding Figures:
Section 2 of the Basic Waltz

Following Figures:
Section 2 of the Basic Waltz (the woman will start outside the
    man on Step 7)

Whisk

Preceding Figures:
Section 3 of the Basic Waltz
Reverse Turn
Hesitation Change

Following Figures:
Chassé from Promenade Position
Wing followed by Progressive Chassé to
    the Right
Hairpin from Promenade Position

Checked Natural with Reverse Pivot

Preceding Figures:
Section 4 of the Basic Waltz
Outside Change
Natural Turn around a Corner
Chassé from Promenade Position
Reverse Turn Chassé
Weave

Following Figures:
Reverse Turn
Reverse Turn Chassé
Three Walks Curving to the Left
Progressive Chassé to the Right
Section 4 of the Basic Waltz if
    following a Checked Natural with
    Reverse Pivot at a Corner

Natural Spin Turn

Preceding Figures:
Section 4 of the Basic Waltz
Outside Change
Natural Turn around a Corner
Chassé from Promenade Position
Reverse Turn Chassé
Weave

Following Figures:
Section 3 of the Basic Waltz
Hover Corté
Section 2 of the Open Telemark Group
Hairpin

Hover Telemark

Preceding Figures:
Section 3 of the Basic Waltz
Reverse Turn
Hesitation Change

Following Figures:
Chassé from Promenade Position
Wing followed by Progressive Chassé to the
    Right
Hairpin from Promenade Position
Weave (if the Hover Telemark is underturned
    to end moving along the zag towards the
    center line)

Hesitation Change

Preceding Figures:
Section 4 of the
    Basic Waltz
Outside Change
Chassé from
    Promenade Position
Reverse Turn Chassé
Weave

Following Figures:
Reverse Turn
Three Walks Curving to the
    Left
Reverse Turn Chassé
Open Telemark
Progressive Chassé to the
    Right
Oversway starting with Steps
    1–3 of the Reverse Turn or
    the Three Walks Curving to
    the Left

Progressive Chassé to the Right

Preceding Figures:

Checked Natural with Reverse Pivot (when dancing along the side of the room)

Wing

Hesitation Change

Section 2 of the Open Telemark Group

Following Figures:

Section 1 of the Basic Waltz

Natural Turn around a Corner

Natural Spin Turn

Three Walks Curving to the Right

Checked Natural with Reverse Pivot

Hesitation Change

Steps 1–3 of the Natural Turn followed by the Open Impetus Turn

Steps 1–4 of the Progressive Chassé to the Right followed by the Open Impetus Turn

Hairpin from Promenade Position

Preceding Figures:

Outside Change ending in Promenade Position

Whisk

Hover Telemark

Open Telemark

Weave ending in Promenade Position

Following Figures:

Section 2 of the Basic Waltz

Outside Change

Outside Change ending in Promenade Position

Open Impetus Turn (overturned)

(N.B. The woman will start outside the man on Step 1 of the above figures.)

Wing

Preceding Figures:

Outside Change ending in Promenade Position

Whisk

Hover Telemark

Open Telemark

Weave ending in Promenade Position

Following Figures:

Progressive Chassé to the Right

Reverse Turn (for the man, Step 1 will be taken outside the woman's left side)

Reverse Turn

Preceding Figures:

Section 2 of the Open Telemark Group

Checked Natural with Reverse Pivot (when dancing along the side of the room)

Hesitation Change

Following Figures:

Section 4 of the Basic Waltz	Whisk
Hover Telemark	Oversway (after Steps 1–3)

Reverse Turn Chassé

Preceding Figures:

Section 2 of the Open Telemark Group

Checked Natural with Reverse Pivot (when dancing along the side of the room)

Hesitation Change

Following Figures:

Section 1 of the Basic Waltz	Natural Turn around a Corner
Natural Spin Turn	Three Walks Curving to the Right
Checked Natural with Reverse Pivot	
Hesitation Change	

Steps 1–3 of the Natural Turn followed by the Open Impetus Turn

Three Walks Curving to the Left

Preceding Figures:
Section 2 of the Open Telemark Group
Checked Natural with Reverse Pivot
(along the room)
Hesitation Change

Following Figures:
Steps 4–6 of the Reverse Turn
Progressive Chassé to the Left
Hairpin
Oversway

Open Impetus Turn

Preceding Figures:
Steps 1–3 of the Natural Turn around a Corner
Three Walks Curving to the Right (if the Open Impetus Turn is
overturned and the woman takes the first step outside the man)
Progressive Chassé to the Right (if the Open Impetus Turn is
underturned and the woman takes the first step outside the man)

Following Figures:
Wing followed by the Progressive Chassé to the Right
Weave
Hover from Promenade Position

Hover from Promenade Position

Preceding Figures:
Open Impetus Turn
Outside Change ending in Promenade Position
Hover Telemark
Open Telemark

**Precedes (N.B. The following figures may be under- or overturned
to resume the appropriate end alignment.):**
Open Impetus Turn
Steps 4–6 of the Natural Turn (woman takes Step 4 outside man)
Steps 4–6 of the Hesitation Change (woman takes Step 4 outside man)
Section 2 of the Basic Waltz to end on a zig

Weave

Preceding Figures:
Open Impetus Turn
Outside Change ending in Promenade Position (overturned to
end moving along the zag towards the center line)
Hover Telemark (underturned to end moving along the zag
towards the center line)
Open Telemark (overturned to end moving
along the zag towards the center line)

Following Figures:
Section 1 of the Basic Waltz
Natural Turn around a Corner
Natural Spin Turn
Three Walks Curving to the Right
Checked Natural with Reverse Pivot
Hesitation Change
Steps 1–3 of the Natural Turn followed
by the Open Impetus Turn

Weave ending in Promenade Position

Preceding Figures:
Steps 1–3 of the Weave

Following Figures:
As for the Outside Change ending in Promenade Position

Oversway

Preceding Figures:
Steps 1–3 of the Reverse Turn
Three Walks Curving to the Left

Following Figures:
Chassé from Promenade Position
Wing followed by the Progressive Chassé to
the Right
Hairpin from Promenade Position

Additional Information

The following organizations will be able to provide you with information about standard ballroom dancing in your area.

Fred Astaire International
407 Bloomfield Avenue
Verona, NJ 07044
(201) 239-1200

Arthur Murray Dance Studios
677 Fifth Avenue, 4th Floor
New York, NY 10022
(212) 935-7787

National Dance Council of America
P.O. Box 2432
Vienna, VA 22183
(703) 281-1581

Arthur Murray Dance Studios
262 North Beverly Drive
Beverly Hills, CA 90210
(310) 274-8867

North American Dance Teachers Association
P.O. Box 85
Vienna, VA 22180
(703) 938-2709

Acknowledgments

The author and publishers would like to thank the following for their participation in this book:
Elaine Bottomer, Michael Burton, Julie Glover, Trevor and Naomi Ironmonger,
Tanya Janes, Camilla Laitala, Jeff and Teresa Lindley and Debbie Watson.

Dance shoes provided by Supadance International Limited.
Practice skirts provided by Chrisanne Creatives. Evening dresses provided by
After 6, Consortium, Tadashi and Vera Mont.